And Blackberries Grew Wild

Susan Ward Mickelberry

ROADSIDE PRESS

And Blackberries Grew Wild

Editor: Michele McDannold

Roadside Press
Colchester, Illinois

Table of Contents

Dedicated to my parents,
Richard Henton Ward, Jr.
and Flora Williams Ward

When I Was But a Child

When I was but a child, I saw the Red Sea
After a long journey down the
mountainside.
And blackberries grew wild
And people planted them
New in their gardens.
"Be still" said a voice
"Be free."
And the berries struggled
And the gardens had snakes.
"But then get up and go forward."
And from the dock,
With the snakes that could talk
With thick green moss on the pilings,
One predicament after another,
With gulls flying overhead.
Ha! Ha!
I gazed out over the sea.

Circumscription of Light

In the late cold mornings that do not belong
anywhere, in gray army housing on
the California coastline, a little boy
named Rollo pedals a red tricycle
through the street, the revolution of each
wheel small and complete.
Nine o'clock in the morning; at twelve o'clock

his mother makes him a grilled cheese sandwich
and he disappears into a dim hallway.
Across the street the little girl stands behind
dead bushes holding cold wet underpants.
She buries them. No one watches
as she sits against the sides of buildings.
Four morning hours. Four in the afternoon.

Inside with the lovely smile, the mother.
During the day she moves rhythmically
toward lunch and the return of her husband
at five o'clock, keeping faithfully
the schedule of the sun. She plays solitaire.
She plays canasta. She smokes filter-tip
Tareytons.

Beneath a white morning canopy
a day begins that does not stop. Time
is bypassed. Very small and very sure,
the child, feeling her own fine bones,
knowing that the cold falling of the sun
is not a part of her. But she does not know
what she knows as she centers in the
long white light.

1950

Under a low morning moon, a bright melody.
The shades are drawn, and there is no light
in the room. The radio is playing
"Slow Boat to China," playing "bonga, bonga,
bonga, I'm so happy in the Congo."
Through the slim light under my door sift
all-important sounds that become the impostor
birds in pantomime outside the window.

Mother, writing letters in another room,
you pulled the shades fast in your children's rooms,
so that they would sleep on and you would have time.
How I love them you thought as you slipped
past their beds to close out the light.

And you really meant it. But love
never has been met at its own level,
and you took a last loving glance,
and turned back to the wide
silent rooms full of light.

Inside her room a child wakens
She pulls a blanket to her chin
and begins early to discover
the dark field of memory.

Apology,
Or
Appreciation Of Someone Else's Life

Envision the silver plane through white clouds
(William Carlos Williams horsey clouds)
roses on a bright wire fence.
Touch a rose with your hand.
Feel the membranous separation
of blood
       and word.

If I so avidly say I hope you have a good trip
       or a wonderful summer
because I like or admire you,
I know
it will not happen because I wish it,
but because of who you are,
       because
you will make it that way.

Peony

When the snapdragon
has always been your favorite flower
and you see your first peony

your heart wilts
like the flower itself in your hand
if you pick it.

There is a simple agony
at the offering
of such unwarranted beauty.

You think of all the most beautiful
women, dark eyes inclined as the flower's,
destroyed in succoring wars,

the veined arches
of their bare white feet
torn open.

Moving

It is a day. Slowly under the black summer tree
I blow deep open holes in the air.
I am moving, and it is hard to remember
where I have been.

Every day the noise is loud.
At night my husband turns on the radio
while I mark hours on the bed with charcoal.
Sometimes in the night he moves close
behind me, wrapping tight his legs.
We are fragile. Held lightly in our place.

Mornings, my little girl pretends
her dolls are animals. I watch her
and pull in
and try to breath.

The Conversation

At the party last night, she was talking
to me. She embroidered my cheek
with her fingernails. I don't know what
she drew; it could have had

something to do with wars.
If only I understood what
it was she was saying. Maybe she
didn't want anything, although her face

was old and jutted with intent;
but I thought she embossed the ridges
of battle, horrid jewels of the tribesmen,
and today I discover, in a different language,

a garden, etched, a thin tracing
of beaded scars, hedges
scrolled into my cheeks like age.

The Sieve

A few afternoons of light in sun
I knew you as well as any—
your face lined as the earth's,
as old.

And now you say
you "thought that I knew you."

The earth a sieve,
I did not.

Last Night I Sat Alone

Last night I sat alone waiting for you
on the ground in the sun under the oak,
as I had waited long ago.
The wind rustled the trees and the
undergrowth.

I drew with a stick in the sand
what looked like a Mayan temple.
My white t-shirt reflected the last sun.
I waited, but you didn't come.

A black dog came out of the woods
and caught me unaware. I waited,
but you were caught up in your living
and had forgotten me.

The wind blew over my shoulder.
Near me the raspberries grew.

Night in the Country

Stepping into a trailer
in the middle of nowhere
in a shapeless open yard
under night stars,
I desire to stay here,
in the morning to go out into it,
to be taken up by the ragged grass
and hungry air.

Now under your wild, moonlike face,
your television face, tying into
limbs unfamiliar as prehistory,
our awed, strange bodies
want it over and over.

Next, the desolate
ride home from nowhere.

Bahamas

Over the oceanic airways
I hear your voice
so clear and blue; you
must be in an open room,
with a balcony.

Tonight you tell me
how I'd like it there,
the sun, the trees,
that it would remind
me of Africa.

You sound
so nice
like you could be in someone's living room,
in the Midwest.

Oh, balcony,
living room,
what is one to do
anyway?

Keyboard

His head moves up and down over
the words, his cheeks flecked with black.
The keys spit out a thousand words
as his body wraps around the typewriter.

His eyes are the lost granite
roosts of his mind.
The room is a cave; table
vibrates like a jackhammer.

The River

He went down the river Sunday with his ex-girlfriend.
Ex from two and a half years ago. She wasn't ever his
girlfriend really, just someone he had the hots for some
three or four months, and whose breasts he wrote about.

He went tubing down the river with her and some
friends. It was the Itchetucknee.

I had gone there with him once. It was supposed to be a
nice day, but it was terrible, filled with ghosts from each
of our pasts and from our pasts together.

They went down the river early, after a long night of
partying. I don't know what it was like. Maybe it was
good. Maybe it was bad.

She has a boyfriend who works at a recycled records
store. He was probably there, too, on the river, but he
doesn't know.

One time I went over to John's house, that's their mutual
friend, and the bottom of her bathing suit was hanging
from his hippie-style chandelier. It was hanging there
in the incense and African reggae — not overly brief, but
white.

14

That was two years ago. Last weekend they went
down the river together after a long party.

I asked this hippie girl out on the Plaza if she had
seen him at John's and, in trying to remember, she
mentioned this other thing. She's a nice woman, with
hair and impetigo on her legs.
She said she didn't go with them—maybe she had to
stay home with her kid.

The river is green and clear. When we went there it
was beautiful, and I drifted naked in the river.

I don't know how this has happened, you can see that.
He doesn't either.
Maybe it was him. Maybe me. Maybe the river.

From Tom in Chicago

From Tom

Having a wonderful time.
Wish you were here.
Bus ride up was insane.
Endless puke and vomit
roiling in my brain—all
our arguments
repeating themselves.
Got off at every stop to see
if I could find a faster
way to get here.
Bo and Mary are fine and
we're having a GREAT TIME.
ALL OF US.
Chicago is a wonderful place
to have a great time.
Been here since Wednesday.
It's Saturday now. Wrote you
a rotten letter on the bus.
Full of all the puke and vomit.
Enclosed.
Write or call me if you want,
but not with more death.

No more death.
Next stop Watervliet. Next stop
the Detroit Grand Prix. Next
stop Little Point Sable.
Love, Vomit, Death, V.D.

Reply

Take your letter,
and your point of view,
and your long journey which
is a "delicate thing,"
and all of your friends (Spoadie
and Robin and Mark) and their sisters
and all of your old airline tickets,
and throw them in Lake Michigan,
along with your head,
which you say you have torn off
in frustration.

Reply

No reply.

I Loved You

At first I loved you,
for being an asshole,
for being insane.
The man before you
ate bananas and cheerios
every a.m. for 18 years.
The one before him
watched T.V. afternoons
in baby blue pajamas,
legs out in front
on the coffee table.
You went to the Bahamas
right after I met you
and brought me
a lucky monkey.
One of those nights we
stood outside your trailer
under the pines
in the moonlight.
Just before I drove away
under the starlight
I said asshole, you asshole.

Now the lucky monkey
lies on my night table
on top of a book,
like a sacrificial pile.
He is made of green rubber
with a red face,
an apple in his right hand.
Earlier tonight, I left a
note on the seat of your car
on white notebook paper.
Asshole, Asshole.
Later I drove past your car
in the parking lot
of a local bar. You did not see me.
You were wearing a white shirt
in a puke green car.
I could see you were insane,
under the moon, you were
an asshole. I loved you.
I drove away.

At the Horse Farm

Canyon of clouds,
horses grazing
in a darkening field,
acrid, lovely smell
that maddens the
buzzing horseflies,
black trailing of leaves.

The horses' legs are lost
in the high weeds.

On the Plaza

Brass and silver
earrings from Brazil,
coconut shells and jaw
porcupine quill.

Silver from Thailand,
stones from Peru,
intricate danglies 3 inches long
red, black, silver, white, blue.

Eyes of God, vine flowers, ampersands
on a blanket in the sand.

Women in long dresses,
men with pale knees.
All a tease. At ease. At ease.

No Attic-ese.

Earrings, red stones, fish bones.
Pirarucu. Pirarucu.

Lochloosa

We'd been walking for an hour in the woods near Lake Lochloosa. The light streamed through the trees intermittently. It pooled around us from time to time. I kept looking for a clear path, but only noticed hints of animal trails here and there in the dense undergrowth of bushes and scraggly trees. Russ was in front with a machete, laughing and swearing occasionally. He was wearing a t-shirt with the sleeves cut out of it. The sweat glistened on his shoulders and arms, and broken pieces of leaf clung to him. He kept brushing away mosquitoes and swiping at the trailing moss.

The path must be in his mind, I was thinking at about the time I saw the beginnings of a clearing ahead.

How often had this happened before, the two of us hiking in impossible terrains, me blindly following. It was funny, really, what a fool I was. And yet we were never lost. What was it I trusted? His vast experience at not getting lost I suppose.

"There it is!" He yelled, already at the clearing's edge. I caught up with him and saw the old shack not far away.

We started across the field. The grasses were yellow and knee high. The high sun turned them white in places. It was noon and we were finally there.

Nightjar

Whippoorwill, whippoorwill, whippoorwill
The trailer is open to the swamp night.

A man lies sleeping on the trailer floor.
We are not together the way we once were.

It is so dark in the dark here,
no moonlight drifts through the open door.

Insects, goatsucker whir in the night;
Night sounds fall into flight.

Whippoorwill, whippoorwill
He says my name out loud.

Into the somnolent night.
I feel the shape of his word.

Asymmetry of couch, stone, brain.
The night air is as damp as stone.

The trailer hangs around us in the night.
We are here inside like terrain.

He touches my foot.
Whippoorwill.

Having Let You

Having let you slip away,
as I am preparing to sleep
this thought of you strikes terribly

anew, perceived through
black water, transparent
yellow of mid-day

as terribly
as a stone from the sky
an old memory revealed.

I know it will not
be said
and put it aside

and gather to me
feathers of the pillow
empty spaces of the bed.

I Would Like To Lie Still . . .

1

I would like to lie still
in bed with you till death,
wrapped in the sheets,
white as a cocoon.

We would barely move,
we would not make love,
we would lie intertwined,
gently holding one another.

Occasionally,
you would touch my face,
I the back of your head,
my lips might brush your chest.

The bottoms of my feet
would rest on your arches.
I would like to lie still with you.

2

We would lie so still
while outside
the voluptuous garden
bloomed.

Next season it would not
be planted. The children
would finish
growing and leave

falling away from us.
The dog would die.
The birds would gather
around the house, singing.

The cardinals, sparrows,
mockingbirds,
bluejays, the gray
catbirds singing.
The black crows.
The wind would blow
past the windows
sweep the wisteria

and the high pines.
Our lives would wither
as our fingers
locked together

one at a time.
I would like
to lie still
with you forever.

Latticework

You want to know about the rest of my life
as we catch the bright rays of winter air
upon the striped towels, on the matted leaves.
Above a jet trails white on a plaster sky,
the trail weaving eventually
into the filigreed white undersides
of branches, white on white lattice work.
Men have passed in and through my life like
rain. It's this late age. Not exactly
that it goes along with pasta, TV-
mediated news and Hefty trash bags —

I mean, every man jack of them has given
me flowers. I haven't directed myself
towards spiritual enlightenment, at least
not since the first of them talked me out of it.
It always seemed there was something to do,
some place to drag my family towards.
Now, after this long twenty years of
contemporary normalcy, seventeen
years with one, three with another,
the door opens on another twenty.

Lately, I've taken up with this hippie
dude. Dude. Now there's a word for you.
I mean, here I am. Getting into it
with an ex-Viet Nam acid-head hippie.
Then last night, when I was in the back room,
someone came into my house. The way it
happened was I kept hearing the noises,
got scared, and went out to find my front door
wide open. I called up the dude and kept
him on the line while I walked through the house.
After I checked and then locked up, he offered
to drive over. When I said "no" he said
he'd call back in twenty minutes. Instead,
he fell asleep listening to National
Public Radio.

I'm thinking about
moving to New Orleans and taking up
Mardi Gras. I'm planning twenty years
of uninterrupted spiritual assertion.

Going to Work

I drank my coffee this morning.
Then on the way to work I hit a dog.
When I got to work, I thought about wearing perfume
and getting a haircut.
I finished my coffee and turned on
the air conditioning because it smelled bad in there.

Later, I watched a fat lady walk toward me
wearing tight red pants.
I went out for a walk and saw a girl in
red dolphin shorts.
I thought about buying a t-shirt
because I saw it in the window when I walked past.

Later, I stopped for a croissant. I thought about
hitting the dog. I thought about how I had fantasized
carrying the dog up and down the street,
but how I had actually found the owner right away
out walking.

When I got to work my hair was still wet
and I was an hour late.
Ce n'est pas.

31

Brazil

It's so wonderful
when someone talks to you like they love you.
It's so sweet.

And you whisper near the back of their head
into the limey air,
the soft curve of their ear.

People, ones who don't know how to love,
will look at you as if they've just come back
from or are just going to Brazil,

or as if they know foreign languages and
understand baseball. And all you can do
is rearrange your clothes

and go home. The sun is so hot
and you wonder if it's worth it,
and about how people get where they do

and how you haven't changed since
you were a kid, and you wonder
about the curves of people's ears

and about how people who ride
buses are always so beautiful in
the strange light there.

Pillar of Salt

It is 6:00 p.m.
The sun still shines on the grass across the lake.

An ibis skims the water, a fish in
its beak, and croaks its low sound, askew.

Dragonflies dart and zoom randomly
in black grass.

On the east side of a lake not far away,
a channel opens. At the end of the channel,

there is a trailer at the edge of a swamp off a long,
dirt road.
A man who lives there tends a ragged garden

and has filled the spare room with marijuana plants.
All the windows in the trailer have broken with use
and age,

doors broken, floors stained with fish blood, his
blood, grease, beer.
Alone for days, now years, he takes long walks
through the swamp.

He watches a black-and-white TV, sports or movies,
listens for the finch whose nest is stuffed between a
broken window and screen.

From a rocking chair he walks in filtered light, through
crumpled
sheets of paper, to a half-open refrigerator.

His neighbors are in trailers scattered up the road:
Mr. Plant, graying
ex-man-of-the-cloth, who borrows beer, whose family
has left him;

Don Foster and Hugh Foster, Hugh, with his black dog,
Hugh, who talks grandly, steals beer, is schizophrenic.

On his walks the man observes the swamp—the low-
hanging moss, hawks and pig
skulls, red ant colonies drifting on rotted cypress logs.

Or he walks to the end of the channel and gazes over the
lake
toward the town in the distance.

"It's always better," he has said,
"to face west across lakes."

Turning away, I see through pale lids, the grass,
insects, palmettos,
beginning to whiten and calcify.

Mrs. Whitfield

Mrs. Whitfield
looked like Jack Benny.
The man sitting in Bageland —
right in the middle of Gainesville, Florida
just north of the prairie-lake that used to
have Buffalo —
looks like Mrs. Whitfield.
Two inches of skin show between his pants
and socks.
His wristwatch is square. He hunches a
little at the waist.
A line of cars is parked under the trees
across the street.
Some children get out of a large brown car
looking like gangsters.
I saw them earlier on the plaza down the
street. They wander in
wearing tie-dye t-shirts, holding tennis
rackets.
I haven't seen Mrs. Whitfield for years.
She lived down the street from me in
Greensboro, NC.
My children used to sneak short-cuts
through her back yard.

The man in Bageland is leaving. His face is
squarish.
His gray-brown hair stands up on his head
like a barbed-wire cloud.
The only place he looks like Jack Benny is
the eyes.

My Cat

My cat isn't really my cat.
I suppose that's not true,
so I've started out
right off telling a lie.

He's been living with me
for five years now. After Russ died
white cat lived in the country
before moving in here.

Every night now he stands on my chest
and looks me seriously in the eye,
and I know he is God there,
white in his fur,

confronting me with my life.
"We are so tied to the dead,"
he says, and I feel my heart
contract in my chest.

My eyes well up,
my throat mimics my heart.
"You are here on the earth,"
he says, "and I see you.

I'm here every night to remind you
of what you know
and what you don't

that you can touch God,
that death is peaceful
that I too will leave
and not come back."

His white fur is his crown
a light blazing behind it.
He is heavy on my chest
so I know he means it.

"That you can make a fist
with your hand and punch
it through the opaque sky
and, perhaps, understand.

It's so easy. I am there,
You see."

How it Went

Oh
God,
I was so much
in love.
In the way it can happen
when you are old enough
to know just too little.
So alive though, so awake. On the precipice.
And that day, we were driving down
to his grandmother's, who was sick,
and I would meet Lynne and Woody
his parents.
We didn't talk much,
content to drive,
together.
Just driving down to Apopka
on Highway 441.
Out of time.
I would glance at him
And see
clear presence.
Joy. Terror. Imbalance.
I wish I could remember the details.
How the road looked. The country.

That beautiful, lost, found
drive down the divided four lane.
I only remember
being together. Happy. Unhappy.
And I remember
arriving
at the upscale motel,
walking into their room,
and how they looked.
Woody, an aging George Peppard.
Lynne's hair so white. Stunning.
Beautiful. Hopeful. Surprised.
Loving, steadfast, crazy,
upbeat, and waiting.

My Poor Little Vain Spirit. . .

I am slogging here in the spectral shift
of all millennia that have passed,
the minute to minute,
and thought to thought,
of all of it.

Stuck
in the middle of a day
in a public bathroom,
I wear a nonsensical pink dress,
and the nanoseconds just race away
this way and that,
from the figures and patterns
of the dress, from
curious skin and hair.

The microcosm of body
dematerializes, on Tuesday,
and my atoms
hover, and race, and
spit, and try to form mind
in a room with a
standard sink.

Oh, my small large mind
expands and beats
like a mockingbird's vulnerable wings
clutches at the porcelain with its claws
yes, aimlessly clutching,
desperate for a stronghold,
grasping
no thing.

Dear Pen

My wrist is stiff,
my fingers frozen.
I am counting on you.
Let it flow.
Let words appear in ink on the page.
Let meaning appear.
Spill my restless heart,
my shadowy soul
on the page so I can see them,
so I can see more
than I think I see.
This field. This heart.
This mottled history.
This to and fro.
Oh, Pen,
to you falls the difficulty,
the unruly task
of lifting the shadow
of our blind eye.

Lust

Desire has come down heavily
upon me, like an eagle,
and threatens to carry me away.

Desire, that golden-winged eagle,
clutches me from above
lifts me barely under shadow.

Oh desire, you are no eagle.

Bitten by the snake
my limbs flow with poison,
this roiling paralysis.

Desire —

These places you lead me —
into the sun's bitter warmth
into the broad mind of a godly man

into dark
coarsely-scarred
corridors

into a ritual,
lightning,
lust.

Yoga Is Hard Work

I am standing on one foot
trying to hold on to my knee.
Meanwhile
the story of my life
is playing out in front of me,
and I am trying to see
what is happening.

It is difficult
as I try to follow the narrative.
I don't want to miss anything.
It takes all of my focus and concentration
not to fall, especially because
over there my first child is being born.
My husband is somewhere else.

My balance gets worse. I focus on a spot
out in front of me. I shift to the other foot
hoping no one will notice.
I wonder if I'm cheating,
work hard not to fall.

A loud voiceover
tells me to swim into the lake,

a puzzling instruction as I can't
see a lake.

Now the story has shifted ahead.
I have missed part of what happened.
In this segment I'm climbing
awkwardly out of a swimming pool.
My children have gone.
What else has happened?

Almost ready to give up,
I try once more
to stand on one foot,
waving my arms about
to see if it will help.

My leg begins to shake
and suddenly
I fall swiftly into my life,
though much of it is missing now.
I see the lake so swim into it as I was told.
Now I am falling in love and
following a man through the forest
watching his back and shoes.
He is walking further ahead,
almost out of reach.

I get back out of the lake
and begin again to stand on one foot.
My teacher is standing next to me,
also on one foot.
He asks me where I have been
and my brain seems to quiet
and I relax and try to breath in breathe out.
And think that everything will be much
better now,
if only I can stand on one foot.
Perhaps it will be easier,
but I am not convinced
as I am still dripping wet

and I am worried about my children.
And hoping I won't fall.

One Tooth

When I died
And went to heaven

I saw
The one tooth
Was a Gucci.

And
She disemboweled me
Proudly.

And the
Scent-laden
Tendrils in the arch
Under your arm

Trail down as if from the sky
Before the sunlit
Backdrop of the window
And anoint the cat
With vision.

51

I Spy Myself at Play

After Rumi

In lotus pose,
eyes closed,

I have been observing you intently.

My eyes have faded away from lack of use,
since my visions are self-created
and don't require the touch of sight.

You have been dancing in my mind space—
climbing trees, in cafes, walking beaches,
experiencing everything you have ever
written,

desired, imagined, played, and fantasized,
seeing and wanting everything
that I know is not me.

I open my eyes
and notice I have wiped you away
allowed a drift of sand to sweep over you

as I witness myself, only a figment, creating
you. And I find I don't know you,
whoever you are.

I only know myself
and my own terror.

Om namo bhagavate vasudevaya.
Om namo bhagavate vasudevaya.
I Om to consciousness.

I will allow myself to manifest
only as consciousness.

After all, it is only the world that you want.
And who would deny you it?

Pausing

Pausing that morning
She was aware
Of the silence and the emptiness
Of the sweet house she lived in.

She was about to go
on a trip to Ohio to visit a friend.
The family was sleeping.
She was alone

With her thoughts, her worries,
In the early light as the sun filtered
Into the space and she looked around
At the walls, the fireplace, the glass

In the windows, the furniture,
The streaming dust in the air, the light,
The expanding light, and
she thought, as she peered ahead,

a window had opened into freedom
into her future, her needs and wants
and potential.

Her first trip away from the life she'd
Randomly built with the loved ones,
The steadiness.

It was she here
With only her life, her ego,
Her intuition and passion looking out.

And she thought she saw fragility
And absence, the great open Yaw.
She thought she saw everything.

A thrill of fear ran through her
As she paused, feeling a sure headiness
And stepped out the door.

How dangerous is revelation
Without understanding, or knowledge,
Or experience.

Wave, Particle, Sex

My lover is a Renaissance man,
witty, joyful, and tonight
we lay naked on the bed, talking,
or rather, me listening, he talking.

And this time it's about
Alan Watts, great Zennist,
and he likes to be expansive, words
tumbling out
as he considers
the universe forgetting what it really is…

And we talk and listen, he and I,
and then we come close, and I feel his body
hot as an oven
and he asks me again to tell him how I like
it, how to please me.
Its endemic among men,
this wondering….

And then we draw closer and he whispers
heavily
in my ear throughout,

and after, it's thank you baby, thank you
baby,
you are the best, you are the best,
you make me crazy...

And we collapse away from each other
roll onto our backs, laughing, laughing,
sated, and free... legs untangled but
touching

And then he begins to talk about infinity:
quantum mechanics, black holes, string
theory,
and all of deep deep space....

And I think how wonderful it is
to lie in bed
naked and free

Listening to your lover
talk about the cosmic Self
playing hide-and-seek

Listening to him talk about
The beginnings of the universe.

Midsummer

On a warm morning
I rest in the shade of a broad oak.
Above, a wasp worries the leaves.
Across the yard two blue jays
argue in a pine.

Midsummer.
In the side yard
a mockingbird mid-medley.
Great silence.
Mourning dove.

In lotus, I see a fly land
on middle finger
of my left hand.
I shake it off.
It finds another finger.

Silence.
Mind empties.
A gentle letting go.
Silence.
Silence.

Where is the cat?
Sweat trickles down my sides.
Grand Central.

The sweet body mind.
Silence.

Aaah.
The cat appears.
Aaaah.

Regret

Sandi is in the hospital, in the ICU.
She's an artist—she and Harold are from
NYC.
I like her voice—it's loud and friendly
And she laughs a lot.

I seldom see them. The last time
I saw Sandi, a few weeks ago,
peeking through her door,
she said she used to have a red milk can
but it was stolen from their yard.

I saw Harold this morning
wandering up their driveway.
He is 89, and looked forlorn.

I went to check with another neighbor,
Reece, to see if he knew about Sandi,
but he wasn't home.
I stand looking at their house, the yard, the
road.

Sandi's red milk can is gone.
Although I never saw it.

Today their yard is still,
With a series of round shrubs
along the edge of the driveway,
And a brilliant white swan planter.

The Tip Top Café

They all shoed their way through the door
High-heeling or sneakering to breakfast house
counters and stools,
Shirting up to tables.
Shoe-stringing their orders to a light-footed waiter
Noting his shiny wingtips a'clacking
As he relished their menu choices.
And they trousered and necklaced into conversation,
Belting and socking and heart-pining,
Setting the
    cafe a'twittering,
Tables fast cluttering, colorful
With plates, forks, eggs, toast,
Sugar spinning, spoons bouncing,
They, aglow with hilarity,
And chatter, ankle straps, boots,
Toes, feet angled under tables and chairs,
Elbows, hands, arms gesticulating,
Faces painted, decorated, brown, pink,
Girls summering in birds and florals,
Guys au courant, hep, shuffling,
Hair blousoned, long or chic, wildly loving
As they laughed frowned churlishly barking
Into the day, immersing themselves
Deeply into the immediacy
Of the café.

Afternoon at the Beach

Early on someone said
"Don't feed the seagulls."
Tide is out. Beach
endless. Bright white
rollers in the deep green.

It's too crowded here. A lady
facing us, reading, a couple
to the left with a dog. Women
draped across lawn chairs.
College group in a circle with a bright
red windcatcher.

After several trips to the water,
that seemed forever far, getting
slapped by the waves,
back on the blanket. Bright sun,
cold water and wind. Our skin burns.
The wind wears us away, eyes stinging.

A lone seagull is circling.
He catches my eye. He is intelligent.
I reach for the chips.
The single gull dances for me, I grab

a few chips and lead him away,
20 feet, 30, and fling them
out and up.

Oh, he loves them, cramming his beak.
I race to the blanket, complete, joyous,
as the throngs arrive, circling, fighting,
screeching around us.
My friend is reading aloud from Thoreau.

The one-footed one arrives. I watch
him, and stretch out my hand
and fingers, as if to say, something. He
pauses, hops about, but finding nothing
but sand,
soars,
up and away.

Flora's Trip

Flora is my mother's name
As a child I didn't know it meant flower
She was named after her great aunt
Who lived out in Oklahoma.

As a child she went to visit there
It was early in the thirties
The roads were two-lane and narrow
It was a long way from Miami.

She sat in the back with her sister,
Mary, but she can't remember
if her sister, June, was born yet
and riding in the car with them.

They stopped in Fayetteville, Arkansas,
to visit her father's relatives
who lived on the outskirts there
out in the Ozark hills.

Just barely a shack on a hillside
Twelve by fourteen she remembers
The women slept inside on pallets
The men on cots under trees.

From there on out to Muskogee
Where my grandfather grew up in
Oklahoma
To a small farm out in the sticks
Not much to call home there either.

She remembers it was the year of the
locusts
And there wasn't even an outhouse
So she and her sister Mary
Had to run across the yard to the cornfield.

They grabbed each others hands fiercely
And ran terrified and laughing
Across the yard with the snapping locusts
And the nights were very dark there.

From there they went on to Minnesota
To visit my grandmother's folks
And then back to Miami
A long trip for children.

On the way back she remembers
They stopped at a motel somewhere

She thinks it was Tennessee
And her dad had driven late.

They piled into a small cottage
And were just falling asleep
When the train flew past yards away
As if it were coming through the room.

They all leaped from bed
Not knowing where they were
Having not known about the train
Confusion in the middle of the night.

They continued home the next day
From those two weeks on the road
The four or five in the car
Young family I never knew.

What a great thing to remember
From seventy years ago
Those things so large and mysterious
They never go away.

Ocean Isle Beach

It's January. The southwest wind
blows past the old pier
holding on in the tidal estuaries
where I sit in the still, late
morning enjoying the sounds.
Gentle rush of incoming tide
creating a lake around the pier,
but soon to recede to oyster flats.

Distant surf pounds the beach
on the ocean side of the island,
across the inland waterway past
the inlet.

The rush of wind freshens
across my face, and
far away I hear the echoed
pounding of hammers, like
African drums.
Cumulus clouds billow
overhead, shades of grey and
silver filtering sun.

Looking around, I note the
absence of big water birds
(white, grey, blue, green)

in the marshes,
only occasional tweets and
whistles, a mockingbird echoing
silence in the Live Oaks.

Suddenly nearby, a ruckus!
Crows descending, circling and
Cawing, and I turn my head just
In time to see the great blue take
off, heavy and slow, out of the
flats where he rested, ascend in
a long turning flight, displaying
his wet, streaked plumage as he
rises, majestic. I lean my head
back on the aged grey bench
to watch.

My soul rests quietly here
in this gentle pooling of tides
midst the tiny sparkling fish,
brown and green marsh
grasses, the buzzy trilling
of flitting wrens,
feels grateful for this pause
in a long life,
waiting only for the tide to turn.

Pieta

My husband's best friend once
Got up in the morning and
Told me he'd had a dream.

I was broken and he was
Carrying me in his arms
Trying to save me,
Wandering around the city
Desperate and grieving.

War of the Worlds

Construction cranes are everywhere,
Even in Starke, Florida,
Where there is so little else.
Where have I not seen them?

Even in Starke, Florida,
Where H.G. Wells never trod,
Where have I not seen them,
These ominous Martian-looking machines?

Where H.G Wells never trod
Down these arid Southern highways
These ominous Martian-looking machines
Overwhelming everything.

Down these arid Southern highways
Where there is so little else.
Overwhelming everything,
Construction cranes are everywhere.

In Bucha

A
bicycle
crashes
down,
ever
flattened,
ghettoed.
Human
innocent
jerks,
killed,
legs
mangled,
now
over,
perished
quickly,
road
shot.
Terrorized
Ukranian
village.
War
X,
Yield
zero.

Before the Party

I was out in the yard
with the cat
waiting for friends to arrive.

I watched the cat's nose
mildly twitch as she smelled
the evening air.

Then came shouting from across the street
out of the dark, like a fist,
a man's voice suddenly rising, yelling
loud, angry, vibrating, louder and louder,
screaming.

My heart surged afraid to beat,
then beating fast.
I envisioned the small wife, the eight-year-
old son.

And then came sounds of impact, like a
pounding on walls.
And me, running fast to the edge of the
street, "You two cut it out!"
I yelled. "Cut it out! Stop! Stop it right now!

Stop! Stop! Stop!" at the edge of the street.
And I heard diminished voices lower some,
and then more.
And I backed again into my lawn, heart still
racing.

And a sudden memory came from long ago
of a poetry workshop with the famous poet,
who suddenly, and for no clear reason,

rose from his chair and backhanded
his girlfriend sitting next to him.
And the circle of people sat in the chairs
stunned into silence.

And no one moved or spoke. And the class
went on.
And the memory of it hung around me in
my yard,
as well as other memories, too many.

As I waited, still shaken, for my friends,
I wondered if I should be afraid.

But in the following hours and days and
 months
no more violence from across the street.

Yet still I hear my words hanging in the air:
"Stop, Stop, Stop."

Friends

Here we are gathered
around the table
celebrating Cinco de Mayo.
Who will return again?
A few of us may have a year or two,
perhaps four or five.
Who will hit 100?
So it is with all my communities.
So many have left already,
no longer walking here.
Who would have guessed?
Not we, who have run free and wild as
words,
we who have loved hard. Performed.
Fought bitterly. Stormed. Laughed.
Regretted.
Lived so many
indescribable lives.
And, so, we take photos,
or lie on couches,
or walk to the ends of the earth, scheming.
As if we could figure a better way.

Or, today, celebrate the unknowable,
raise glasses to the tilt of the earth.

May it always be so.

The Stoplight

I am stranded at a light.
The turn signal blinks for a left turn,
making the loud, echoing ticks of a clock.

Across the street a row of live oaks
is laced with Spanish moss,
backlit by the bright gold of sunset.

I have the sudden thought
that in another time
I would not have lived so long,

affected as I am with
high blood pressure, half blindness,
and various random maladies.

The air outside is cold. Later
I will be somewhere else. Just right now though
I experience the strangeness of being in this time,
this place,

this particular set of circumstances that is my life,
and I wonder how it would have played out,
my body, my face, my own gray brain,

in some other century, I, born some other way,
for some other reason, with some other eternal goal,
or peculiar intent.

The Birds

My cat is chattering
at the robins.
Outside the window
they have swarmed
with their booming
songs into the yard
green from rain and
are scattering
everywhere, to
delicate tree limbs,
the feeder, porch roof
and skylights,
skittering bird feet
hopping on the roof.
And they are feeding
in the lawn, running
and attacking with
their little beaks.
Fifty or so swoop up
from the azaleas
and cherry laurels
across the pale sky
and white clouds,
as still more arrive.

So quickly so quickly
they swoop and
swarm. And then most
are gone, as quickly as
the changing light,
leaving only a few stragglers
behind to throw berries
loudly onto the porch roof.
And Anabel,
the cross-eyed tabby,
meowing and chattering,
looks up, aroused,
looking out through the glass
from her own various perches
at this startling phenomenon,
the migratory birds. Her chatter
unexpected and thrilling,
an echo of wildness
in her home-bound life.
Each pounding of the berries
on the metal rooftop alarms.
She climbs up next
to me and my book
and lets me rub her
neck. And the light
changes again as the

last straggler leaves,
as all the molecules
of dust calm, and
even the squirrels
and cardinals
return, life an
intimate puzzle,
and evening silence
begins to approach,
and life is all around us
as Anabel and I look
out the window.
And we wonder at it all.

Snow

It has been snowing all day.
It is shockingly beautiful,
shocking. It shocks the mind
awake. Everything is white.
I look out a window.
The trees, the shrubs,
a blanket of white.

My love has gone from this world,
I have come to this place to grieve him.
I grieve. I grieve. I sleep. I grieve.

I read The Tibetan Book of Living
and Dying. As light fills the window
I fall into deep sleep. Deep. Deep.

My love comes to me in a dream.
He slashes with a knife.
Again. Again. A knife. My blood
red, though only in a dream.

It's okay, I say, into the dream,
it's okay, intently,
holding the pain,

which is only his love, and as I
love, the dream fills up, fills with love,
love fills my dream.

And the dream goes on for a long time,
like snow.

Open, Shut

I am standing on the porch
of the house I came home to
when I was born. In old Miami
where my full-bodied grandmother
rocked me on the porch swing,
snuggling me to her bosom.

Open shut, open shut.
Sleep little baby.

I'm looking at the
black and white
photo of myself
time bombed
my platinum hair, short,
gazing over my left shoulder
down the street toward the avenue
and Allapattah
past the pony rink on the corner
across the band field and
the high school.
The coconut palms around the yard.
The wringer washer on the back porch.

Caught in the beauty of
the always astounding moment.

Open shut. Open shut.
Sleep little baby.

Knowing then, and every day after,
the only thing I'll ever know.
Every moment is a lifetime.

Flying to Asmara

I am deep in the bucket seat, small,
my mother beside me
holding my brother
who is two and a half.

It's cold and I am wrapped in a blanket.
I hear the loud plane engines, and smell
a metallic smell everywhere. Soldiers are
scattered around, some walking in the aisles.

My dad is behind us, singing softly, sounding
like he's on the radio. He sang as he carried me
onto the plane, "Baby it's cold outside."
And snowing, the white flakes all around us.

Outside the little windows, I can see the clouds.
Sometimes they bring us cold chicken in boxes.
My mom is patient, silent, and quiet
exhausted from holding my brother in her lap.

He's funny sometimes, he wants to know
what the clouds are, and would like to
touch them, he thinks they look soft
and wonders why they are floating.

We've been flying a long time
since the last time we got off the plane,
beginning in New York, then Greenland,
the Azores, Tripoli, Cairo, Eritrea.

Once when we get off the plane
we have to run to the hotel through
a sandstorm that stings our skin
and we are all screaming.

My dad is running too
shepherding us to this distant place
where he will be adjutant at a military
base, called "Radio Marina."

A 1950s outpost of America
the Beautiful, an outpost of the
Cold War, high on a plateau
above the Red Sea.

Two children and parents flying in Military Air
Transport planes
across three continents and oceans. Across a lifetime.
To a beautiful, magical place. Just a beginning.
None of us knows what will happen.

Everything

Everything seems to be
moving toward me.

at a steady speed.

Until it gets close, and
then it slows down.

And then it comes right on in.

It doesn't seem to be in my body.

Where did it go?

Acknowledgements

Thank you to the following publications in which some of the poems in this collection previously appeared.

Flora's Trip, Brazil, and The Stoplight: *This is Poetry Volume IV: Poets of the South*

Having Let You and Afternoon at the Beach: *Melrose Poetry Anthology*

Nightjar: *Blue Moon Review*

The Conversation: *Florida Review*

Moving: *Via I,* UC Berkely

Susan Ward Mickelberry, born in Miami during WWII, has lived around the continental US and in Africa, where she spent several childhood years in Asmara, Eritrea, an event that colored her life. She earned an MA in English Literature from the University of Florida and lives with her cats in Gainesville where she worked as an editor and writer at UF. A lifelong student of ballet and dance, she teaches yoga and participates in regional poetry readings and events, including PoJam, the longest running open mic in Florida. Her poem "The Conversation" was Finalist in the Florida Poetry Contest at the *Florida Review*. Other poems appear in *Blue Moon Review, Via I, Greensboro Review, Florida Quarterly, The Melrose Poetry Anthology, This is Poetry, Volume IV: Poets of the South, AC PAPA No. 3*, and others.

Author Photo by Tristan Ford Frower

Susan Ward Mickelberry's poetry presents a "microcosm of body"—an intimacy of sensory experience found in whippoorwills and windows, fish bones and raspberries, mosquitos and moss, blood and thorns, a standard sink, a red tricycle. But this intimacy of detail, along with gentle rhythms of Mickelberry's narrative voice, cannot distract from the sheer breadth of content carried in the poetry. Reading her poems is like stepping into gentle waves of one of the beaches she writes about—the crispness of the water and sand and other minute sensations is vividly alive within the context of the vastness of the ocean itself. This collection moves from Apopka to Asmara, Muskogee to the Bahamas, the Ozark hills to Azores, exploring themes of "Everything"— love, sex, fragility, loss, abuse, revelation, consciousness, voice. *And Blackberries Grew Wild* offers us the unpretentious but rich and evocative life experiences of a deeply honest, thoughtful poet.—J. Nishida, Poetry Editor of Bacopa Literary Review 2024

MORE ROADSIDE PRESS TITLES:

MORE ROADSIDE PRESS TITLES:

Nothing and Too Much to Talk About
Nancy Patrice Davenport

Bar Guide for the Seriously Deranged
Alan Catlin

Born on Good Friday
Nathan Graziano

Under Normal Conditions
Karl Koweski

Clown Gravy
Misti Rainwater-Lites

Walking Away
Michael D. Grover

All in a Pretty Little Row
Dan Provost

These Are the People in Your Neighbourhood
Jordan Trethewey

Radio Water
Francine Witte

They Said I Wasn't College Material
Scot Young